1. You are not alone ...

*

*"I put off going to university by taking a year out to do voluntary work. Then I did a course I hated for a whole year (maths) because I couldn't make up my mind what I really did want to study. When I finally got my degree, I did a postgraduate course to postpone making a career decision—and when the end looked perilously close, I went abroad to teach English for a year so that I wouldn't have to write my thesis for a while. After six months of writing up, I was more confused than ever, so I applied to do a PGCE, but by the time I'd finished that I thought I'd just try one more thing before settling down to life as a teacher. So I got a job in publishing. Sometimes I think that I only go to work every day (to edit, among other things, this **Just the Job Handbook**), to put off deciding what to have for dinner."*

Not-so-recent French and philosophy graduate

Some kind words of reassurance. Some harsh words of realism.

It's never easy to grapple with life's big decisions. Sometimes even minor, everyday decisions—where shall we go on Friday night? what can I get my mum for Christmas?—can result in hours of paralysing doubt. So it's hardly surprising that what looks like the biggest decision of your life—the choice of a career—should have caused endless grief to generations of students and graduates. This handbook has two simple aims: to help you become less clueless than you are now, and to make you feel more in control of the process of choosing a career. What it won't do is to make any decisions for you. Neither this book nor your best friend can do that for you.

So if you lack a clear direction and are feeling puzzled by the choices available to you, here are some reassuring facts that should make you feel better. *

Some reassuring facts

Uncertainty is normal

It's very unusual, in my experience, to meet someone who knows exactly what they want to do with their lives. Even those studying vocational courses like medicine or law can be assailed by doubts. And tabloid newspapers just love lurid tales of nuns and priests who abandon their vocation for a life of freedom, sin and normality.

Procrastination is normal

At 4 am most nights during term time, you can guarantee that a substantial proportion of the student population is beavering away at an essay that was set three weeks ago. Don't tell me these people are going to change overnight when the graduate recruitment fairy waves her wand and turns them into accountants or civil engineers. There wouldn't be a huge industry in time management courses and books if people did everything they promised to do well in advance of the event. Avoiding making decisions is not very bright but it is normal.

*

"I went overseas two weeks after my last exam with no real plan except to keep my options open. Science, my degree subject, was definitely not for me. In Hong Kong I applied for whatever job I saw and almost ended up managing a café in a posh hotel, selling insurance door to door and training to be a shipping clerk for an import/export company. The job I eventually accepted was in a specialist scientific publishing company. I fell into publishing by chance, but it's by design that I'm still there."

Science graduate

Of course it's better to start earlier but...

Ideally, everyone should begin to plan their future at an early stage. But very few people do. It takes the edge off the fun of going to university to be worrying about distant and serious events. Unfortunately, what tends to happen is decisions get taken in an atmosphere of panic at the most unsuitable time of all—the months before final examinations. It's always better to start thinking as early as possible but, whenever you begin, don't panic—it's never too late.

Feeling better? Good. But knowing that you are not alone in feeling confused, however comforting, does not actually help a great deal in moving things on. The next step is to spell out some slightly more painful truths.

Some home truths

Career decision-making is a process

It's unusual for people to fall into a career. There are certain simple measures you can take to make your choice of a career as logical as possible. It's tempting, and a damn sight easier, to trust in fate and to impersonate a leaf being blown along by life's breezes, but I wouldn't recommend it. Some people are lucky in life but most of us have to make our own luck. *

You must look inwards as well as outwards

This is the tricky part. We are not a nation of navel-gazers. Self-analysis is almost as painful as root canal treatment. In other parts of the world they love talking about themselves, but in the UK and Ireland we prefer to talk about the weather. But self-analysis is not a luxury; it is the basis of all sensible career decision-making. Sometimes in life you just have to grit your teeth and do the difficult thing. Afer all, you are responsible for your own life. Yes you, no one else. You are the world's expert on you. No one can, or should, make decisions for you.

Summary

- Don't be too hard on yourself.
- It's natural not to have a clear idea of what you want to do and it's natural to seek to put off thinking about it.
- But you can't stay natural for ever ...

2. Current realities

The changing world of graduate employment. The implications for your career.

Let's just pause a while before considering the processes of making a career choice, because choosing what to do with your life is not an activity that takes place in a vacuum.

Over the past few years there have been many fundamental changes to the nature of work itself that need to be taken into account before you start making plans for the future. And so it is with graduate recruitment too. The changes are far-reaching and either totally scary or pleasurably challenging, depending on your point of view. I advise you to lean towards the latter because, scary or not, these changes are happening and you will have to deal with them positively.

How the world of employment is evolving

Large employers are changing

In the past, a significant number of graduates found their way into large, well-known organisations in the public and private sectors. These days are gone, probably for ever. Even the giants of graduate recruitment are advertising fewer jobs and therefore it's becoming more competitive to secure a job with the best-known organisations out there.

There are more opportunities in smaller organisations

The real growth in job opportunities is taking place in smaller organisations. But because they lack the high profile and advertising budgets of the recruitment giants, it's not always easy to notice this. *

Some small organisations are full of graduates and have been created by smart people who have left large organisations to set themselves up in business. They need graduates to help them grow. Other equally successful small businesses have rarely, or

*

"I always swore that I'd never work in an office. I wanted to be creative, work with people and all the other clichés that slightly pretentious arts students exchange through clouds of cigarette smoke. But when you graduate, the air clears, the harsh realities bite and you just have to find a job. I now work in sales and marketing for a small company—in an office— and the atmosphere is great. We wear jeans to work, go to the pub (no alcohol though) at lunch time and generally have a laugh when we're not too busy. The work is surprisingly creative too. We're nearly all young graduates and sometimes it feels like I'm back at college. My friends who found work with the big, traditional graduate recruiters have found the transition to working life much tougher."

Recent history graduate

ever, taken on a graduate. This is not because they have anything against graduates. Rather, it's because in the past they never needed to. These organisations will rarely offer a structured training programme but they can provide early responsibility and, to the individual, a sense of being involved in the heart of the business rather than feeling like a small fish in a big pond.

The structure and the nature of work is changing

As organisations become leaner by losing staff, management structures inevitably become flatter and this has obvious consequences for your career development. One of the consequences is that the notion of career progression being a slow and steady climb up a ladder has become the exception rather than the rule. Progression is now as likely to mean a move sideways to take on a new and often quite different responsibility. *

It may be possible, without changing your employer, to pursue several separate careers in your lifetime. Work is likely to be more social too, with project groups from many disciplines coming together to work on specific tasks. These developments mean that in order to be successful at work you will need to expect change, learn quickly and work effectively in teams.

Working life is set to become unpredictable with many of you being employed on temporary contracts. There will be fewer "jobs for life" and much less job security in many areas. There will be an increasing flexibility in working patterns. * * Technology will mean that more people will work from home. There will be more people sharing jobs and working part-time. More people will have more than one job or start their own business.

The graduate job is not easily defined

A graduate job used to be something that was easy to define. Nowadays, however, it may prove easier to get a job than to pin down the concept of graduate employment! This is largely due to the continuing expansion in higher education and the changes to working life that I have already described. In the future, graduates will be working in jobs that were once considered to be beneath them in some sense. But don't be future, graduates will be working in jobs that were once considered to be beneath them in some sense. But don't be despondent. It was only relatively recently that retail management was thought to be a respectable career for a graduate. And whatever you do, console yourself with the thought that the "training to think" provided by a degree should give you a head start and the edge over non-graduates.

The individual (yes, that's you!) takes more responsibility

These seismic changes mean that, more than ever before, you yourself need to take the major role in your own career development. With more frequent job changes, less job security, fewer formal graduate training programmes, greater opportunities in small companies and the gradual demise of hierarchies at work, you have an opportunity to attempt to manage your career in a way that has never been possible before. But in order to do so, you need to develop the appropriate skills. And this leads us nicely to a crucial step: looking at yourself.

Summary

- Work is changing and traditional linear careers are getting rarer.

- You shouldn't rely on others to shape your career.

- Try to develop the career management skills that you will need for as long as you work for a living.

"Some people slip through the net. They have the skills we're looking for, but they haven't thought about whether they really want the job. That's why the very last part of our selection process is half a day in a store. It isn't a big glossy sell—sometimes we put them in our worst stores. We find that it helps both sides to decide."

Philip Horn, ASDA

3. Looking at yourself

Skills. Values. The importance of skills and values. Looking on the bright side.

We are all different. We might look the same or we might be studying the same subject. We might even enjoy the same music, but each of us is a unique blend of skills and values and it's vital that you understand who you are and what you want. *

A few words about skills

As far as career choice is concerned, the first thing you need to clarify is what skills you have and which ones you wish to develop. Now the whole skill thing is quite an emotive topic. Some people might say that lists of skills are in fact instruments of torture dreamt up by careers advisers who have no idea of what a real job is ("Are you sure you have the evidence for the interpersonal skills and teamworking abilities you need for that job as a hermit?") in collusion with employers who have clearly never met a real person ("Ambitious self-starter with drive and initiative wanted for position as receptionist"). ✱

✱

"If it's any consolation, there are some employers out there who hate those CVs that begin with a 'skills profile' or 'mission statement', apparently generated randomly by a computer. They appear to reduce a perfectly normal person to a character in a novel consisting entirely of lists. I occasionally help to recruit graduates for the small software company and scientific consultancy that I work for. My boss bins all the CVs, which don't show how the 'skills' fit in with the 'experience'."

Physics graduate

OK, so some of those skill words *are* jargon. But that doesn't mean you should ignore them. If they're the language of recruitment, you should learn it. After all, you wouldn't expect to live abroad without picking up some useful phrases of the local lingo. Classifications of skills may be arbitrary, but they are a genuinely useful tool for looking at yourself with a view to a career.

Think of the skills stuff as a game, if you like. And let's be honest: if I'm writing this book and you're reading it, we must both be playing in some sense. There follows, for what it's worth, my version of the rules. I can't claim that this is original. It's based largely on a recent report by the Association of Graduate Recruiters, but that only makes it all the more valuable. I'd suggest then that there are three main sorts of skills which we all need in our working lives.

1. Work-related skills

In order to do any job reasonably well, you need a collection of readily identifiable skills. A journalist needs to be able to write, a lawyer needs to be able to present complex ideas simply, a production manager needs to be organised, a social worker must be good at defusing tension. We all develop skills naturally throughout life although we rarely bother to write them down as we go along. We don't even tend to identify them. Here are some examples, broken down into four further categories.

Examples	
Specialist	It helps to be an expert at something (eg marketing, tax accounting, family law, aerospace engineering, marine biology, organisational psychology)
Generalist	it helps to have general business skills and knowledge (eg finance/ basic accounting, written communication, problem-solving, use of IT)
Connected	It helps to be a team player (eg management skills, meetings skills, negotiation skills, networking skills, presentation skills)
Self-reliant	It helps to be able to work alone as well as with others (eg confidence, self-awareness, action planning, political awareness—more about this below)

Knowing what you're good at not only helps you to choose between jobs, it also helps you to fill in all those awful application forms and to answer those tricky questions at interview. But it's not that easy to sit down and write a list of your existing and potential skills. The simplest way is to use one of those computer programs available through careers services and the like. But if you're one of those people with a phobia of both computers and careers services, why not just sit down with someone who knows you and generate a long list of your strengths? Further help with this is given later in this chapter.

2. Job-hunting skills

These skills are explained in the other three titles in the *Just the Job* series—*Making wizard APPLICATIONS, FIRST INTERVIEWS—sorted!* and *SECOND INTERVIEWS and ASSESSMENT CENTRES—going all the way!*

You also need a set of very specific skills related to the process of applying for and securing employment. Sad to say, however well-endowed you are with personal skills, you do need to develop job-hunting skills too.

3. Career management skills

Probably the most important skills listed above are the "self-reliance" ones. That's because employers have identified them as the ones you particularly need to manage your career. In today's changing employment world, you need to be able to seize opportunities to influence the direction of your own career. The skills needed for this are listed below and, I would argue, they are the sort of skills that everyone needs to develop.

Examples	**Career management skills & effective learning skills**
Self-awareness	Able clearly to identify skills, values, interests and core strengths. Equipped with evidence of abilities. Actively willing to seek feedback from others. Able to identify areas for personal, academic and professional development.
Self-promotion	Able to define and promote own agenda. Can identify "customer needs" (academic/community/employer) and can promote own strengths in a convincing way.
Exploring opportunities	Able to identify, create, investigate and seize opportunities. Has research skills to identify possible sources of information, help and support.
Action planning	Able to plan an effective course of action. Able to implement an action plan, organising time effectively and preparing contingency plans. Able to monitor and evaluate progress against specific objectives.
Networking	Aware of the need to develop networks of contacts. Able to define, develop and maintain a support network for advice and information.
Matching and decision-making	Understands personal priorities and constraints (internal and external), which includes the need for a sustainable balance of work and home life. Able to match opportunities to core skills, knowledge, values, interests etc. Able to make an informed decision based on the available opportunities.
Negotiation	Able to negotiate from a position of powerlessness. Able to reach "win/win" agreements.
Political awareness	Understands the hidden tensions and power struggles within organisations. Aware of the location of power and influence within organisations.
Coping with uncertainty	Able to adapt goals in the light of changing circumstances. Able to take myriads of tiny risks.
Development focus	Committed to lifelong learning. Understands preferred method and style of learning. Reflects on learning from experiences, good and bad. Able to learn from the mistakes of others.
Transfer skills	Able to apply skills to new contexts—a higher level skill in itself.
Self-confidence	Has an underlying confidence in abilities, based on past successes. Also has a personal sense of self-worth, not dependent on performance.

Taken from *Skills for Graduates in the 21st Century* by The Association of Graduate Recruiters, 1995.

*

"I've given up law twice now! I initially went to university to do law, but found it excruciatingly boring. So I changed to history after a term—and loved every minute of it. After university, I agonized long and hard over career choices. In the end, as I knew I had the right abilities to do law, I decided to take a conversion course after a year off travelling. I stuck it through to the end of my training contract with a big firm of solicitors. Surprise, surprise ... I still hated it! Now I'm travelling again, older and a lot wiser, than the last time."

History graduate

✳ ✳

*"After graduating I went to teach English abroad. At the end of my contract, I returned home and got a job in the media. In many ways I enjoyed it, but I simply wasn't as happy as I could have been. It wasn't so much what I **was** doing, as what I **wasn't** doing. I missed the travel and the teaching. So I gave it all up and I'm headed back to the Far East next month, to help train English teachers."*

English graduate

A few words about values

As well as understanding what you are good at, it's equally important to understand what you want out of work. So examine your values carefully.

Example	**What are you looking for?**	
Adventure	A challenge	Constant change
Security	To help others	To be under pressure
Variety	Travel	
Money	A routine	A social life

The consequences of value mismatches are serious. You may, for example, have the perfect skills to consider teaching as a career but if money is what you crave, then you may end up dissatisfied. If you value your social life, don't join a company which expects you to work 14 hours a day. You may have the skills to do it, but you won't be happy. ✳

Where skills and values fit in

The career choice process can most easily be represented as a continuous cycle of four separate stages. If you like, it's a kind of spiral, which doesn't stop when you get a job, but should continue throughout your career.

Example

Self-awareness
Who am I?

Taking action
How best to apply?

Opportunity awareness
What is available out there?

Decision-making
How can I make the best match?

You can of course start the process anywhere, but most people will begin by becoming more self-aware, because knowing what your skills and values are is a good basis for moving on to consider a range of opportunities. This process is not only valid for recent graduates but also for anyone, at any stage of their life, who wants to develop or change their career. ✳ ✳

Accentuating the positive

Some people respond to the issue of personal skills by robustly asserting that they haven't got any—at least in the form that careers advisers and employers want. Others say that they have the skills but other factors mean that no one will be interested in hearing about them.

You may genuinely feel that you are short of skills but, hang on a minute, are you certain that you have lived your life without being good at *anything*? The great thing about skills is that they are transferable—hence phrases like "key transferable skills". Being good at something in your social life, for example, can be transferred to a potential work situation. Any holiday job you have done, even the most routine, can be analysed for lurking skill content. Every sport or pastime, every bit of travel and maybe even your degree course can conceal skills that you never believed you had.

Examples

Holiday job A routine vacation job serving in a pub, when looked at creatively, can yield quite surprising results. You deal with customers, work under pressure, defuse potentially tricky situations, show numeracy, take responsibility. Break the job down even further and consider how you deal with customers. Are you patient? Can you calm them down when they get restless? Do you make them laugh?

Summer inter-railing Did you show organisational skills in planning the trip? Were you resourceful and imaginative in surviving on little money? Did you encounter and overcome problems?

Unless you have lived the life of a hermit for the last ten years, you will find that all your activities tell you something about yourself. And remember that we often forget the detail of our own lives. It's easy to look back a decade and see a collection of mundane experiences and draw the totally ludicrous conclusion that you don't have any skills. It's not some form of beauty contest where you compare your attributes with someone else's, or a pointless exercise to generate a list of meaningless words. It's a straightforward attempt to understand yourself in terms of competences that are required to be successful at work.

And if you feel confident about your skills but cynical about factors outside your control, then it's your duty to anticipate the objections of others and plan a strategy that will overcome those objections. Here are some examples.

1. I'm a mature student

If you are a mature student, you have probably had the opportunity, through work experience or family commitments, to develop a whole range of work-related skills. But you have to be able to interpret these experiences in terms that employers understand. Bringing up children, for example, may not be immediately relevant to a job in the civil service but if you analyse what you actually did, you'll probably find evidence of good organisational or time management skills and a lot more besides.

2. I have a flawed academic record

If you truly believe that you have the skills necessary to do the job but are worried about dodgy A levels or a failed first year, then your task is to own up and sell yourself. If the organisation is looking for someone with a particular range of skills, be upfront with the academic bad news: "I know you will be surprised to see that I failed my first year. It was a hard lesson for me and one I don't intend repeating. I hope, however, you will look beyond that failure and concentrate on my strengths.."

3. I'm studying at an unfashionable institution

How can you persuade an employer that, just because you are studying at a university that they don't normally target, you should be taken seriously? The best way is to construct an application or CV focused specifically on your skills and experience. But you must be absolutely clear about what you have to offer. You can also try the networking approach explained in the next chapter.

 Another book in this series—*Making wizard APPLICATIONS* deals with CVs in more detail.

Summary

- Knowing yourself is not just for Californians. It is the essential first step in making sense of the opportunities available to you.

- There is a process of career choice that will help you to make informed decisions about your future now and throughout your working life.

4. Looking at careers and jobs

"I left accountancy to manage my dad's company. When that failed (nice management, shame about the product!), I started temping as an accountant again. That led me to my current 'employer', but I managed to negotiate my work on a freelance basis. This means I can work the hours I want—ideal for hangovers. And when I'm feeling rich, I just take off for a week's surfing or mountain biking."

Biochemistry graduate

"When I was a student I bought myself an old ambulance—as you do. It's not that I've got a paramedic fetish or anything, but I saw it as a way of supplementing my ever-dwindling grant—and it worked! I did light removals, shifting pianos, etc. And when there was a college rugby or cricket tour, I bunged some seats in the back and became a bus driver. I carried on for a year or so after graduating and generally carried on making money on a small scale. Then I got bored and took off to Hong Kong to become a stockbroker."

Economics graduate

Sifting through the possibilities. Finding out more. Networking to get working.

Let's start with a couple of definitions. A job is what you do when you're not enjoying your free time. A career is a series of jobs.

These are important definitions because the changing nature of work means that, for most of you at least, a conventional career that involves a linear and logical progression through working life, is probably not on. And this is another reason why you need to develop the skills and desire to plan and manage your own career progression. *

Researching your opportunities

Of course, no matter how much digging around you do in the murky depths of your own personality, no job or career is ever going to suggest itself unless you already know something about it. However much you know about fifteenth-century erotic French poetry or fluid dynamics, it is unlikely that your education so far has taught you much about jobs, unless you are on a super-vocational, double-decker sandwich course. You probably have only a very hazy idea about what your family and friends do at work. And you can't select your options from the limited number of jobs you see in action every day: lecturing, librarianship, shop work, bar work, newscasting, bus driving, etc. ** So it stands to reason that you need to do a bit of active research.

Putting it very simply, the options open to you after a degree are:

- a job
- a postgraduate course
- self-employment
- taking a break
- none of the above.

In each case, you need to do two things: find out more and relate your choices to your skills and values.

Some general points about researching opportunities

There are three ways to find out about anything before you actually do it, and jobs are no exception. First, you can read about them (on paper or on the Internet). Secondly, you can ask people to explain them. Thirdly, you can watch people doing them and even have a tentative bash yourself. This is not a random order. The last way is better than the middle way, which is better than the first way (although it's fine for doing the basic ground work). And guess which way most people choose to find out about jobs? No prizes for that one.

The second and third ways to research opportunities, which involve you talking to other people, are often described as a networking approach. This approach is more fun and more revealing than reading a book (even this one) but requires more effort and time. Many students spend the whole of their vacations getting work experience and making contacts, which is laudable, but not compulsory. I shall deal with networking in more detail at the end of this chapter.

gti You could start on the Internet with *GTI careerscape* at http:\\www.gti.co.uk. It has more information about different jobs than we could possibly list here.

Finding out more about ...

A job

Part of the problem about occupational choice is the range of opportunities available. Whatever your degree, you can apply for nearly half the jobs advertised to graduates each year. So you have to narrow it down in one of—yes, you guessed it—three ways.

The first and most comprehensive method is to look at everything that you could do, regardless of whether you really fancy it or not. Try not to be influenced by stereotypes— accountants are boring, actuaries are more boring, marketing people are flash, social workers wear cardigans, you know the kind of thing I mean—and not even consider how competitive a job area it is.

The easiest place to start is with books and leaflets: careers services and bookshops are full of them. There are also many electronic sources around to help. **gti**

You can also talk to people at presentations or careers events. If all else fails you can usually identify someone who is doing an interesting job and try to speak to them through friends, family or the *Yellow Pages*. There's more about this 'networking' approach later in the chapter.

Remember, the aim of this exercise is to end up with a number of jobs that look interesting. In Chapter 5, I'll explore ways of narrowing this list down.

A postgraduate course

*
"By the time I'd finished my PhD in physics, five years after starting it, I was pretty cheesed off with science. Call me a lemon, but that possibility just hadn't occurred to me when I started. To make matters worse, I'd had a run-in with my supervisor, so my references were a bit dodgy. I didn't want to waste the experience I'd gained though, so I spent a year or so trying to get into scientific publishing, while my contemporaries breezed into post-docs or industry. I was getting pretty depressed, when I discovered those things called patents and the people who write and register them. Now I'm happily training to be a patent officer. If only I'd researched the options open to me at an earlier stage, I'd have saved a lot of time!"

Physics graduate

Sometimes the identification of interesting jobs means that you will have to consider a postgraduate course. You cannot become a lawyer or a teacher without further study, for example. You may also be moved to study further by a desire to learn more without necessarily having a job in mind. But whatever you do, don't fall into the common trap of thinking that further study is an *alternative* to a career. Even non-vocational courses can have a vast impact on your future opportunities. The important thing is to work out what career doors the course will close, as well as the ones it will open, BEFORE you start. * It can be a long fall from an ivory tower!

Finding out about postgraduate study is relatively easy. There are many directories and listings that show all postgraduate courses in the UK and many in the rest of the world. If you have left university, write to your old careers service and ask to be sent a copy. Once you have a short list, you can write to the institutions concerned for a prospectus with more details.

As well as identifying the course, you will need to investigate eligibility requirements, sources of funding and application procedures. Some courses, for example, have more grants attached to them than others, some require you to go through a clearing house while others want direct applications. All university departments offering postgraduate programmes will send you some information.

But don't rely solely on what you read. Judging by prospectuses sent out by course providers you'd be hard pressed to find a useless course. They do exist, so try to speak to people that have taken the course. Ask the admissions tutor what happens to graduates when they leave. Visit the university and look at the facilities. Make no assumptions. Find out before wasting your time and money.

*

*"I always knew that I
wanted to be my own boss.
So when I left university I
got together with a mate
to start our own business.
Trouble was, we didn't
know what kind of
business! We both liked
cars, so we started by
buying second-hand cars,
very old ones, tarting them
up a bit and selling them
on. One day, I was driving
around in a surprisingly
immaculate white Ford
Sierra that I'd just bought,
when I happened to see an
identical car. And when I
say identical, I mean it—
down to the registration
number! The experience
cured me of car-dealing for
ever, but I'll never be cured
of self-employment. I'm in
Mexican food now ..."*

Psychology graduate

Self-employment

More graduates are considering self-employment, and why not?
If you have an idea and the drive, it's probably worth a go soon
after you graduate. You won't have a lot to lose, you're used to
working unsocial hours and, for many of you, it beats working
for someone else. *

But do take advice first. There is a lot of free advice offered to
those wanting to start small businesses, so take advantage of
every scrap. Banks have helpful information packs available and,
generally speaking, helpful staff working in this area. Your local
training and enterprise council (TEC) or local enterprise council
(LEC) in Scotland (address in phone book) licenses advisers to
help you with your plans and stocks plenty of written
information as well.

The essential elements, whether you're in the right-on vegan
food business or writing highly commercial computer games of
dubious moral value, are: thinking about the customers who will
want and afford your goods or services; obtaining the financial
backing; supplying the goods or services on time; and all the
other logistical headaches involved in running your own
business.

If you correctly assess your own talents and self-motivation as
well as finding that proverbial niche ... who knows? Move over
Richard Branson! In no time, you may find yourself recruiting
graduates.

Taking a break

One of your options is to take a break, travel a bit, do something
different, put your feet up for a well-earned break after 15 years
of study. Nothing wrong with that, of course, especially if you
are in your early twenties. You are, after all, looking at about 45
years of working life. It's enough to make anyone leave the
country.

But don't take a break without looking into the issues, which
can be summarised in a series of questions:

• What will you do and where will you go?

• Will you need to raise some money/pay off debts first?

• Why are you doing it?

- What will other people (potential employers) think of it?
- Will it help me to get the job I want afterwards?
- Should I try to get something organised (job/course) before I go?
- When's the best time to return?

Like every other opportunity that you face, this one needs research and planning. Many students intend to take a break after graduation but very few actually do. Taking time out requires a level of thought and forward planning that is slightly inconsistent with the notion of leaving these shores or doing something different.

* *"Most people take one year off. I took ten. All I've ever really been interested in is rock climbing. So when I left college, I went to Sheffield, signed on and went climbing every day the weather was good enough. Over the years, I've had a bit of sponsorship, done some difficult access work, travelled a bit, been in all the climbing magazines, but the pattern has been more or less the same. I'm not rich like all my contemporaries who became accountants, but I reckon I'm happier—and I'm a famous rock star, at least in the climbing sense! Unemployment definitely has its benefits. Next year, I'm taking time out of taking time out to do an MSc. But who knows what will happen after that!"*

Physics graduate

None of the above

One of your options is to do nothing, which is a nice thought after final exams. I can't really recommend this as a long term option because it doesn't suit many people. Unfortunately, however, for some graduates it's a sort of involuntary choice. It's called unemployment.

There aren't many positive things to be said about unemployment but I can think of two. First, any period of inactivity is an opportunity, unasked for but nevertheless an opportunity, to acquire skills that were previously absent or undeveloped. Secondly, because of the changes going on around us in the job market, we can (or should) all expect occasional periods without work. You won't necessarily greet these "career pauses" with undiluted joy but you must use them positively to add to your knowledge and skills base. *****

So what about networking then?

Networking is something we do naturally almost every day of our lives. We meet friends through other friends and in next to no time we have a network of mates. The principle is exactly the same when it comes to developing a network to find out about jobs. It needs a bit more courage but it is not beyond your competence, however shy you are. And while you're networking, you are putting yourself at the front of the queue, if your enquiries about the nature of jobs result in the discovery of concealed job vacancies.

The networking process has the following phases.

1. Finding a contact

We all have friends, relatives and members of academic staff who, in turn, know hundreds of other people. ✳ Your careers service will also have contacts in a range of occupations. Even if you can't find a contact through your own network, you can generally find a name from the phone book or relevant employment directory, by engaging in a bit of detective work or by attending careers fairs and presentations.

Let's assume you want to find out more about drama therapy. Now, as a rule, drama therapists don't visit universities on the milk round and there won't be a huge amount of information in the careers library. You have drawn a blank with your own friends and acquaintances—no one knows a drama therapist. Start by contacting the professional association (nearly every job has one). They will either give you the names of local practitioners or tell you where drama therapists practise. Very soon you will have the name of someone who works locally.

2. Arranging a meeting

The next step is to meet your contact. You can either write with a few details of yourself and why you would appreciate a meeting, or you can phone. If you write, end the letter by saying that you will phone in a few days to try and arrange a meeting. Try to speak to the contact—you may have to phone a few times. When you sort out a mutually convenient time, you must stress three things:

- you are asking for a SHORT meeting
- you are NOT looking for a job, but information about the job
- you have already found out something about the job.

You will be surprised that most people, even total strangers, respond well to phone calls from pleasant, well-motivated students and graduates. If they enjoy their job, they won't mind talking about it—as long as you come across as genuinely interested. This is a basic truth about networking.

Before the meeting, prepare by reading all you can about the job. If you're worried about remembering the questions that you want to ask, write them down and take them with you.

3. The meeting

Remember this is a short meeting, so get straight to the point. Ask them to describe their work—its joys and agonies, how they got in, where they have worked and what the future holds. Ask them for any advice and guidance they can give. Take along your CV. Ask them to suggest things that you could do to strengthen your eventual application. See if they know any other drama therapists in the area that you could talk to.

4. After the meeting

Write and thank them for their time. If you felt a certain amount of warmth towards the person, keep them in touch with your progress. Follow up any of the leads that you were given at the meeting. Before you know it, your network is up and running!

Networking is the single most effective way of finding out about jobs. You can get insights that you could never get from reading a brochure or hearing a talk. Above all, you can get an accurate picture of the skills and values of people in the job, which makes it easier for you to estimate whether you are a credible candidate for this line of work.

Networking can also yield unexpected results. You could get vacation work, a job offer, or you may meet your future employer ... or even the love of your life. By getting off the sofa and going out and meeting people, you are demonstrating a drive and commitment that not many others show. And finally, you can use the networking approach when you are looking for jobs as well as information about jobs. *

Mind you, when you phone to arrange a meeting I would still advise against saying that you want a job. That invites the response: "We don't have any vacancies" and a premature end to your network. The power of networking is in the personal contact, allowing someone else to be personally impressed by your suitability. This gives you a head start over all the other candidates who appear as just so many words on an application form.

*

"I did a vacation placement with the BBC. The people I was working with didn't have any permanent vacancies, so they sent me to have tea with someone who might! As it happens, he didn't either, but he knew someone in magazines who was looking for someone just like me. Unfortunately the magazine (a title about the Internet, about which I then knew nothing) folded after a few months. But at about the same time, the person responsible for running the Web site of a company where a friend works happened to leave. She got them to invite me in for an informal interview and two days later I was starting work—and, yes, being paid for surfing the Net most of the day! It wasn't quite a world wide web that got me here, but it was a pretty complex network!"

Recent English graduate

Summary

- Find out about all the opportunities available to you, preferably by talking to people.

- Network, network, network.

5. Matching yourself to the job

Asking the right questions. Giving yourself the honest answers.

What you should aim for is to find a job that suits your skills and values. If you're honest with yourself, it will save a lot of heartache and wasted time when it comes to filling in application forms. ✱ You can either start by looking at yourself—your strengths and needs—and then looking for jobs that match them, or you can look at jobs that interest you and then see whether you have the necessary skills to do them. Either way, you won't be able to make much of a choice unless you have done the ground work outlined in Chapters 3 and 4.

✱
*"Whenever I see an application which says, 'I am ideally suited to a career in publishing, because I enjoyed my degree in English', I feel like tearing it up. Don't people ever stop to think about **why** they are good at what they do or **why** they enjoy it? I might even invite a train-spotter to interview if they said their hobby offered them the chance to see the world or allowed them to meet a wide variety of people."*

Director, publishing company

Asking the right questions

If you prefer to work from the jobs available, begin the process by picking the most interesting and asking yourself the following questions:

- **What are the main duties of the job?**

  Break the job down into as many duties as possible.

  For example, a journalist will be expected, amongst other things, to write stories, interview people and attend court sessions.

- **What skills are they looking for?**

  Take each duty and calculate the skills necessary to achieve a reasonable level of success.

  Writing news stories requires (obviously) writing skills but also accuracy and the ability to deliver under the pressure of constant deadlines.

- **Have I got most of these skills?**

  Be honest with yourself. There's not a lot of point in applying for jobs that you won't be able to do very well.

  If you lack the required skills, either choose something else or, more positively, do something about acquiring them.

- **Could I persuade someone I have?**

  Believing that you have the necessary skills is fine but you need to prove it to your potential employer.

The best way to prove anything is to point to evidence—times in your life when you have successfully demonstrated the key skills that they are looking for. And remember that skills are transferable from any part of your life and can be used to show that you have the potential they seek. But don't torture yourself. If you have no evidence, it may be that you are looking at the wrong job.

The reality test

There are times in life when things don't go according to plan, and career planning is no exception. You may have all the right skills and experience and be a terrific and magnetic personality but sometimes the jobs you crave are just hopelessly competitive. Or they genuinely don't have any vacancies.

Some idealists are shocked to find that charity work, voluntary work overseas or jobs in conservation can be harder to secure than a graduate traineeship with a merchant bank. You might think you're getting out of the rat race before you get into it, but let's face it, those nice furry squirrels are just rats with fluffy tails—and they're always trying to get to the top of the tree. An alternative route to an "alternative" career may paradoxically lie in the most conventional of jobs. ✱ If you get yourself trained up as an accountant in a cut-throat environment, you will find yourself much more desirable to, say, a charity than any well-meaning graduate fresh from university.

In such cases you have to ditch the emotional baggage and apply the reality test. How realistic is it to carry on? If you can't face doing something completely different from your aspirations, can you do something similar that's easier to get into? The classic examples are selling as a foundation for a career in marketing or working a bookshop to gain useful experience for book publishing.

✱

"I hated the City law firm where I did my training contract. But then they didn't like my monkey boots either. So I did my time, then left to do a year's postgraduate course. Now I'm a law lecturer, which is what I always wanted to do. I don't think I would have got the job without my experience of practising, so I'm glad I did it—if only because lecturing is one of the few jobs where you can be as scruffy as a student!"

Law graduate

Summary

- Explore suitable jobs by looking for a *realistic* skills match.

- Consider alternative ways of obtaining the desired job.

6. Investigating suitable employers and vacancies

GTI careerscape (http://www.gti.co.uk) has employer recruitment pages and links to companies' own sites.

Some useful places to begin your job hunt. Some alternative places to start looking.

If you're still at university, there are lots of careers journals and directories containing information about employers and vacancies, together with details of the job areas that they're likely to be recruiting into. They're excellent at telling you what the medium and large organisations are looking for, but may have fewer ads from smaller or more specialist employers. Most reasonably-sized employers also have their own recruitment brochures and, increasingly, their own Web pages on the Internet.

Graduate vacancies are advertised regularly throughout the year in university careers service bulletins and national vacancy lists. If you've left university you can usually arrange to have them sent on. Most of the big national broadsheets have a day when they advertise graduate jobs, as well as more specialist days devoted to jobs at all levels in specific sectors.

* "I was riding through the university campus on my bike one day, listening to my favourite local radio station on my walkman, when they advertised one of their own job vacancies. They were looking for a commercial production assistant—making and lining up ads to go on air. Although they weren't asking for a graduate, I'm sure the fact that I was about to get my degree in a relevant technical subject helped me get the job and, after a year, promotion to the work I'm doing now: making programme links for the whole group of radio stations. Who says you shouldn't have to get on your bike to find a job?"

Electronic engineering graduate

If you're still a student, you may find that your university has a programme of visiting employers, known for some reason as the milkround, where you can be interviewed on campus. This is a hugely convenient arrangement but only involves the larger companies which particularly want to target your institution. It's also possible to meet employers more informally through a series of fairs, presentations and other events that take place during the year: some national and some based at individual universities. Talking to people who work for an organisation is the best way to get a feel for the company culture, just as it's the best way to find out about areas of work. There's only so much that a glossy recruitment brochure can tell you.

You also need to keep your ear to the ground. Some jobs are advertised in the strangest of places and some not at all. * The big, blue-chip graduate recruiters may have a high profile, but they offer only a fraction of the jobs. To find out about less obvious employers, you need to network—as described in Chapter 4. No one knows for certain how many jobs are never advertised but it's a substantial number. And they go, by and large, not to close relatives of the boss but to people who are known to the boss and have impressed him or her with their commitment and energy. These are people who have networked. *

Summary

- Look in the obvious places for the obvious employers.
- Look beyond the obvious places and the employers. It's more work but the results may justify the extra effort.

7. The last word ...

Some final nuggets of wisdom.

To become clued-up from a position of cluelessness demands positive action. It requires effort but it will be worth it. Unless you win the lottery, the chances are you'll have to work for a living, so maybe it's worth a bit of effort to make sure you find a job that makes you want to get up in the morning.

Career fantasies

If it's not too negative I'll finish with a word of warning. Speaking as someone who has built a long and successful career on the issue of careers, I've heard many career fantasies in my time. But these, for what they're worth, are my top three.

1. There is a perfect job for me

There's no harm at all in working towards your perfect job. Who knows, you may get it one day. But a slavish belief in this fantasy will stop you considering all those jobs which you could do well, you would quite enjoy and might lead to your perfect job in the end. * * I'm not saying you should take any old rubbish that comes along, but it's surely illogical to believe that there is only one job in the world that could possibly satisfy you.

2. My first job is critical: my career is my life

The days where graduates joined a company in a particular job area and retired, 40 years later with a gold watch, are virtually

---

*
"I've sort of got two careers. I'm completing my graduate traineeship at a major retailer, but I've also managed to sell some of my knitwear designs to other big fashion chains. The first career fell out of a recruitment brochure into my lap, but the second one required a more foot-in-the-door, networking approach."

Landscape architecture graduate

* *
*"I'm a missionary. Yes, don't laugh, we still exist. I don't look anything like Jeremy Irons, more's the pity, and it's not like you'd imagine it. In fact, it's not like **I** imagined it. I did degrees in science and computing. And then I did a degree in theology to escape from science and computing. But when I got to South America, all they wanted me to do was set up computer systems. I don't really mind. I'm here to help after all, but it's not exactly what I planned."*

Natural sciences and theology graduate

over. Many of you will have several job changes, a few wrong turnings and a career break or two. Even if not, there is life outside work. ✶ You can still do all the things you loved to do as a student: watch soap operas, eat kebabs, live in pleasantly seedy shared houses ... and with any luck you'll have the money to do a lot more besides with your free time. ✶ ✶ And on the bad days at the office, construction site or factory, console yourself with the fact that your first job is not a one-way street to the rest of your career. It's enough that it provides you with enjoyment and the opportunity to improve your skills.

3. I have to use my degree

Is it really a waste of three or four years if you don't use your degree in a job? I don't think so, especially if you haven't enjoyed your studies. The job market is very flexible in the UK and Ireland and it makes sense to explore all your options.

As I said, there are many other dangerous career fantasies ("I owe it to myself to apply for City jobs", "I can't get a job, so I'll apply to do teacher training", "All my friends are applying for milkround vacancies, so I'd better do the same"). I've heard them all. But the three I've outlined above are the most likely to inhibit decision-making and lead to long periods of inaction.

The science of careers?

What I've described in this book is a series of steps that you can take, in any order, to clarify the opportunities available and to make the best possible decisions. But career choice is not an exact science and you might find yourself in a wonderful job surrounded by awful people. You may end up, totally by accident and with no planning whatever, in a deeply satisfying job that you didn't even know existed. You might scheme and plan for months, get a job offer and fail the medical.

There is always going to be an element of luck involved but it would be crazy to trust in luck as a strategy. And the best definition of a lucky person is someone who can recognise an opportunity and seize it with both hands.

✶

"I thought my life would change completely the day I became a civil servant. To make the transition less traumatic, I went out and rented a video recorder to record Neighbours. *But then I realised that life wasn't so different anyway. I could still go to gay clubs, see my old friends and generally have a good time. Five years down the line, I can afford a big black motorbike with all the leather gear. No one at work knows about my other life as a gay biker, but on a good day you can just about see my tattoo through my impeccably ironed shirt."*

Modern languages graduate

✶ ✶

"When asked about her hobbies at interview a friend said she was taking flying lessons. When asked why she wanted to become a lawyer, she replied 'To pay for the flying lessons'. She got the job."

Law student

Summary

- Don't fall for the standard fantasies of careers planning.

- Don't trust in luck. Have a strategy.

JUST THE JOB HANDBOOKS

There are 3 more titles in the Just the Job series.

FIRST INTERVIEWS—sorted!

Perhaps not the most 'scientific' part of the selection process, but an inevitable part of job-seeking. This handbook covers every stage from the heart-stopping letter inviting you to the interview to the bone-crushing handshake with the interviewer as you leave.

'You must believe that you are a good candidate and they must think so too— they don't invite people to interview because they're lonely and need someone to talk to.'

Making wizard APPLICATIONS

These meticulously crafted forms, CVs and covering letters are normally the first contact you will have with potential employers. Buying this handbook is a cheaper alternative than sticking unmarked large-denomination banknotes to the back of the application form.

'Unless you write and tell someone that you are a wonderful person, they will never know of your existence.'

SECOND INTERVIEWS and ASSESSMENT CENTRES—Going all the way!

If you've come this far, they obviously like you, and you hopefully like them. You are close to getting a job, but the fat lady's only warming up ... While you wait, try reading this handbook. It explains what the employers are looking for and how they'll find it—in group exercises, presentations and ability tests. It tells you how to prepare and why you shouldn't panic when you see a clipboard.

'You have a right to be there. So try not to dwell on the other candidates and try not to compare yourself with them.'

GTI also publishes a series of **Careers Journals** that are essential reading for students and graduates. Each title focuses on a major area of work—Law, IT, Engineering, City & Finance, Construction and Food & Drink—and describes the careers available and the routes in. For more information about the *GTI Careers Journals* or other GTI publications look at our web site—*GTI careerscape* www.gti.co.uk

To order *Just the Job Handbooks*, *GTI Careers Journals* or any of GTI's other careers publications:

 Call GTI on 01491 826262 with your credit card number

 Write to GTI enclosing a cheque payable to GTI
(p&p for 1 copy 50p, 2 or more copies £1)

 Order through the web site *GTI careerscape* www.gti.co.uk

GTI Specialist Publishers, The Barns, Preston Crowmarsh, Wallingford, Oxon OX10 6SL
Tel: 01491 826262 Fax: 01491 826401